Science That's Appropriate <u>and</u> Doable

This science resource book was written with two goals in mind:

- to provide "good" science for your students
- to make it easy for you

What makes this book "good" science?

When you follow the step-by-step lessons in this book, you'll be using an instructional model that makes science education relevant to real life.

- Your students will be drawn in by interesting activities that encourage them to express what they already know about a concept.

- Your students will participate in hands-on discovery experiences and be guided to describe the experiences in their own words. Together, you'll record the experiences in both class and individual logbooks.

- You'll provide explanations and vocabulary that will help your students accurately explain what they have experienced.

- Your students will have opportunities to apply their new understandings to new situations.

What makes this book easy for you?

- The step-by-step activities are easy to understand and have illustrations where it's important.

- The resources you need are at your fingertips — record sheets; logbook forms; and other reproducibles such as minibooks, task cards, picture cards, and pages to make into overhead transparencies.

- Each science concept is presented in a self-contained section. You can decide to do the entire book or pick only those sections that enhance your own curriculum.

> For sites on the World Wide Web that supplement the material in this resource book, go to http://www.evan-moor.com and look for the <u>Product Updates</u> link on the main page.

Using Logbooks as Learning Tools

Logbooks are valuable learning tools for several reasons:
- Logbooks give students an opportunity to put what they are learning into their own words.
- Putting ideas into words is an important step in internalizing new information. Whether spoken or written, this experience allows students to synthesize their thinking.
- Explaining and describing experiences help students make connections between several concepts and ideas.
- Logbook entries allow the teacher to catch misunderstandings right away and then reteach.
- Logbooks are a useful reference for students and a record of what has been learned.

Two Types of Logbooks

The Class Logbook

A class logbook is completed by the teacher and the class together. The teacher records student experiences and helps students make sense of their observations. The class logbook is a working document. You will return to it often for a review of what has been learned. As new information is acquired, make additions and corrections to the logbook.

Individual Science Logbooks

Individual students process their own understanding of investigations by writing their own responses in their own logbooks. Two types of logbook pages are provided in this unit.

1. Open-ended logbook pages:
   Pages 4 and 5 provide two choices of pages that can be used to respond to activities in the unit. At times you may wish students to write in their own logbooks and then share their ideas as the class logbook entry is made. After the class logbook has been completed, allow students to revise and add information to their own logbooks. At other times you may wish students to copy the class logbook entry into their own logbooks.

2. Specific logbook pages:
   You will find record forms or activity sheets following many activities that can be added to each student's logbook.

At the conclusion of the unit, reproduce a copy of the logbook cover on page 3 for each student. Students can then organize both types of pages and staple them with the cover.

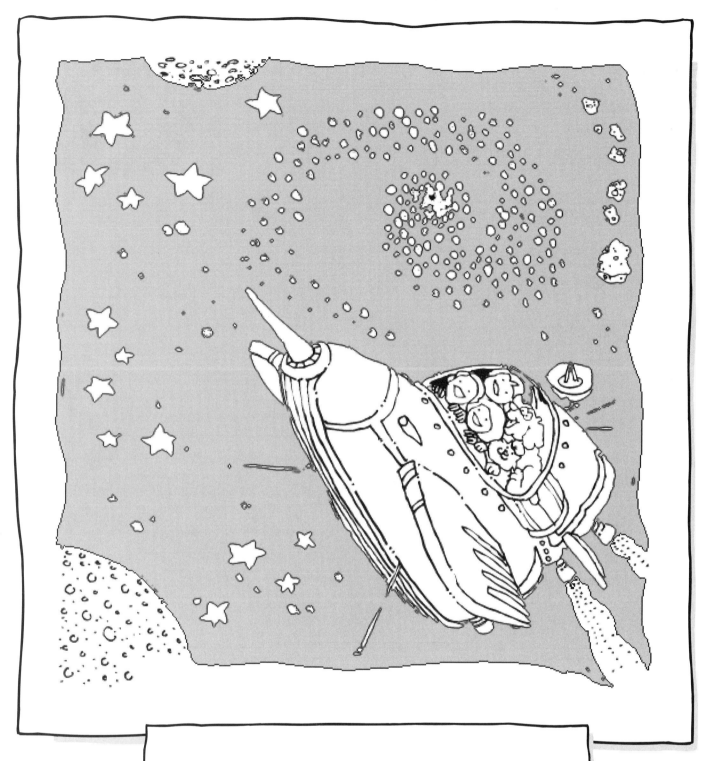

_____'s

Space Logbook

Exploring Space • EMC 853

Name _____

This is what I learned about space today:

Name _____

Investigation: _____

What we did:

_____

_____

_____

What we saw:

_____

_____

_____

What we learned:

_____

_____

_____

Earth is part of a solar system in the Milky Way galaxy.

Teaching Resources

- Before beginning *Exploring Space,* set up a class library. The text of many books on space will be too advanced for primary grade students, but the illustrations and photographs can be used. Read appropriate sections and paraphrase the more complicated material.

- Check your district audiovisual catalog for videos and filmstrips appropriate for each concept in this unit.

- If possible, borrow a model of the planetary system from a high school science department.

Introduce the Solar System

- Take the class outside to see how many things they can see in the sky. List these and others they think of. Ask what can be seen in the sky at night and add those objects to the list.

- With student input, cross out the items that are part of the Earth. Read the remaining items and ask, "What are these things a part of?" If not mentioned by a child, you will need to say that these objects are all part of what we call space and that the Earth is in space, too.

~~bird~~	~~cloud~~	moon
~~airplane~~	stars	~~butterfly~~
sun	~~jet~~	~~kite~~

- Explain that the Earth is part of something called a solar system. Tell students that they are going to find out what else is in our solar system.

  Read an appropriate book such as *Solar System* by Amanda Davis (Rosen Publishing Group, 1997) and *The Planets* by Gail Gibbons (Holiday House, 1993).

- Begin a class logbook with a page entitled "Things in Our Solar System." Start by asking which items on the "What Is in the Sky?" list should be included. Then add other items that students mention. List all responses, even incorrect items such as stars. Corrections will be made as student knowledge increases.

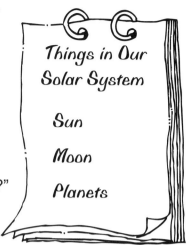

Things in Our Solar System

Sun

Moon

Planets

Gather More Information

- Show films and videos and read additional books, such as *Hello Out There* by Joanna Cole (Scholastic, 1995) to learn more about the solar system.

  Add new objects to the "Things in Our Solar System" logbook page (asteroids, dwarf planets, meteoroids, space dust). Help students recognize and delete any incorrect items.

- Make an overhead transparency of page 9 to use as you review the objects in our solar system. Point to each object and ask students to name it. Ask for a specific name—Mars, not planet, for example.

  Reproduce page 10 for each student to complete.

Solar System Minibook

- Reproduce pages 11–13 for each student. Read and complete the minibook together.

- Work with students to define "solar system." Write the definition on a class logbook page. Reproduce page 4 for students to copy the definition for their individual logbooks.

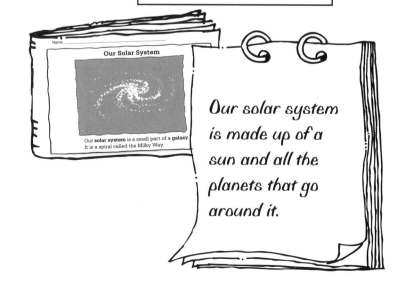

Our solar system is made up of a sun and all the planets that go around it.

Your Place in Space

Reproduce page 14 for each student. Read *My Place in Space* by Hirst (Orchard, 1992). Then ask students to fill in the blanks on their envelope to complete their whole school address.

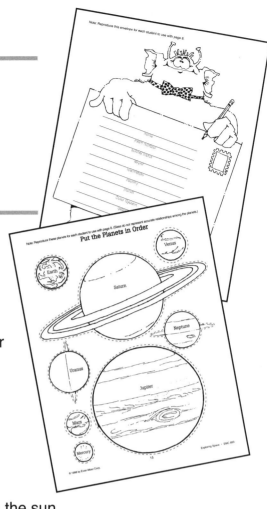

Put the Planets in Order

Students follow the directions on page 15 to paste the planets in order.

Materials

- patterns on page 15, reproduced for each student
- two 6" x 18" (15 x 45.5 cm) pieces of construction paper
- scissors
- crayons
- glue

Steps to Follow

1. Paste the two pieces of paper together as shown.
2. Draw the sun on the left end.
3. Color, cut out, and paste the planets in their order from the sun.
4. Write a title—Our Solar System.

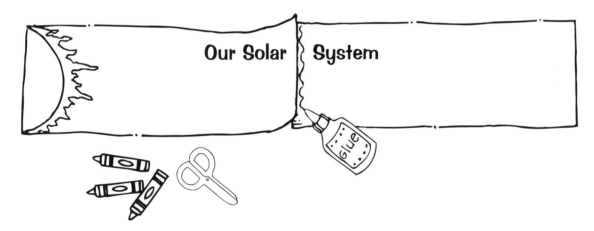

Objects in Space

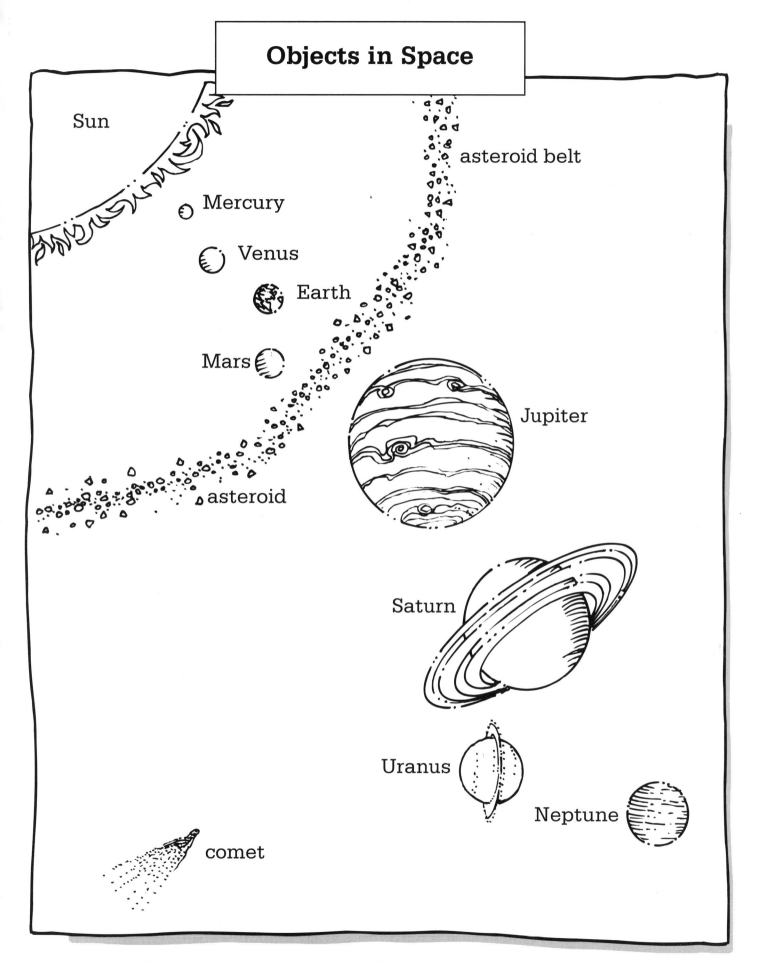

Sun

Mercury

Venus

Earth

Mars

asteroid belt

asteroid

Jupiter

Saturn

Uranus

Neptune

comet

9

Name_____

What Is It?

comet	asteroids	planets
moon	star	Milky Way Galaxy

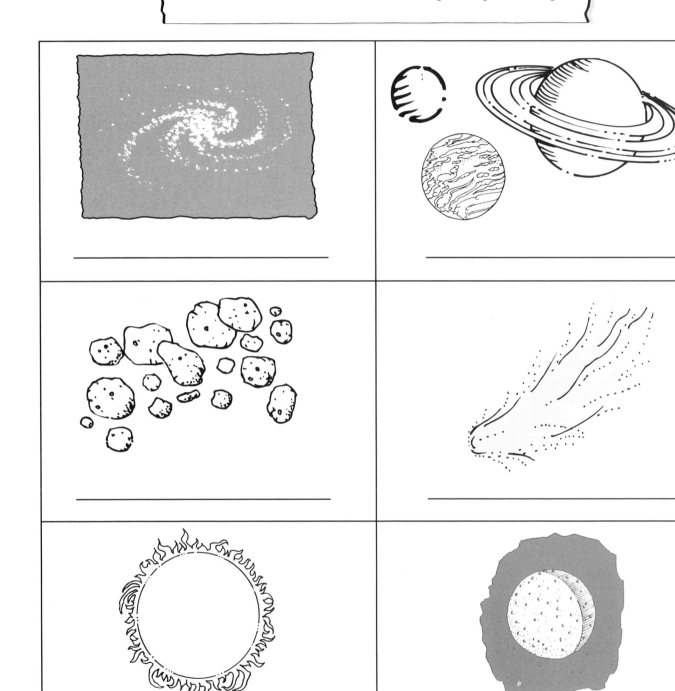

_____ _____

_____ _____

_____ _____

Name_____

Our Solar System

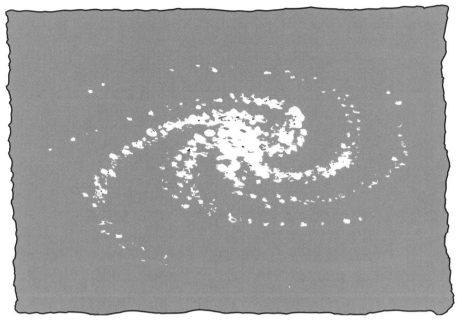

Our **solar system** is a small part of a **galaxy**.
It is a spiral called the Milky Way.

1

sun

planet

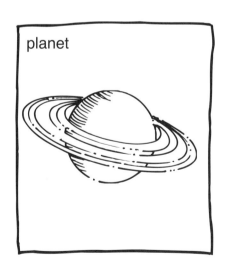

moon

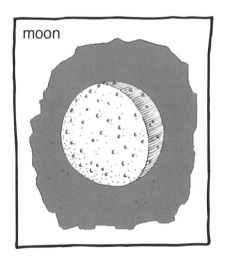

Our solar system has many parts. The sun is the center of
our solar system. Eight planets with their moons **(satellites)**
go around **(orbit)** the sun.

2

There are eight planets in our solar system.

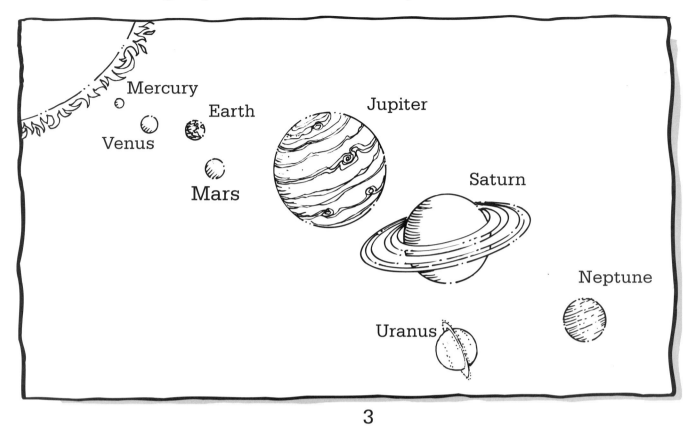

Mercury

Venus

Earth

Mars

Jupiter

Saturn

Uranus

Neptune

3

Planets move in two ways.

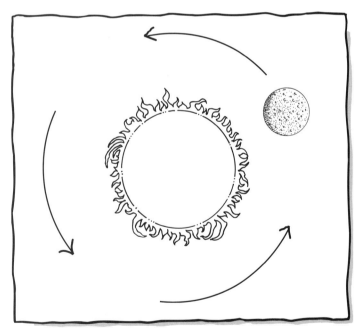

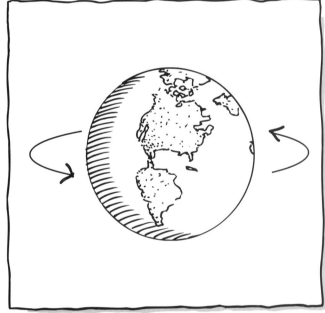

They move around the sun.
Each planet travels along its
own path (orbit).

Planets spin around like a top.

4

Other objects orbit the sun, too.

meteoroids

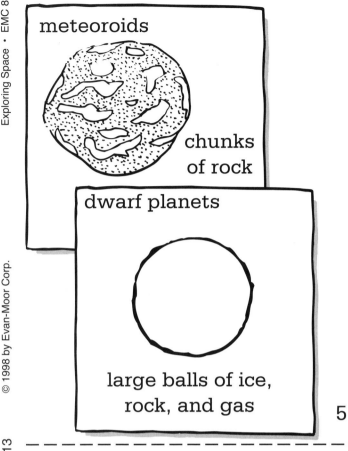

chunks
of rock

asteroids

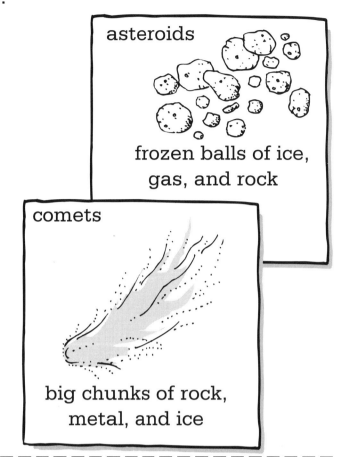

frozen balls of ice,
gas, and rock

dwarf planets

large balls of ice,
rock, and gas

5

comets

big chunks of rock,
metal, and ice

Some of the planets in our solar system are smaller than Earth.
Some of the planets are larger than Earth.

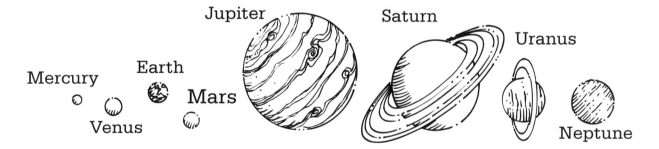

List the planets that are smaller than Earth.

1. _____ 2. _____ 3. _____

List the planets that are larger than Earth.

1. _____ 2. _____ 3. _____ 4. _____

Note: Reproduce this envelope for each student to use with page 8.

name

room number

school name

street

town/state

country

planet

Solar System

galaxy

Universe

Note: Reproduce these planets for each student to use with page 8. (Sizes do not represent accurate relationships among the planets.)

Put the Planets in Order

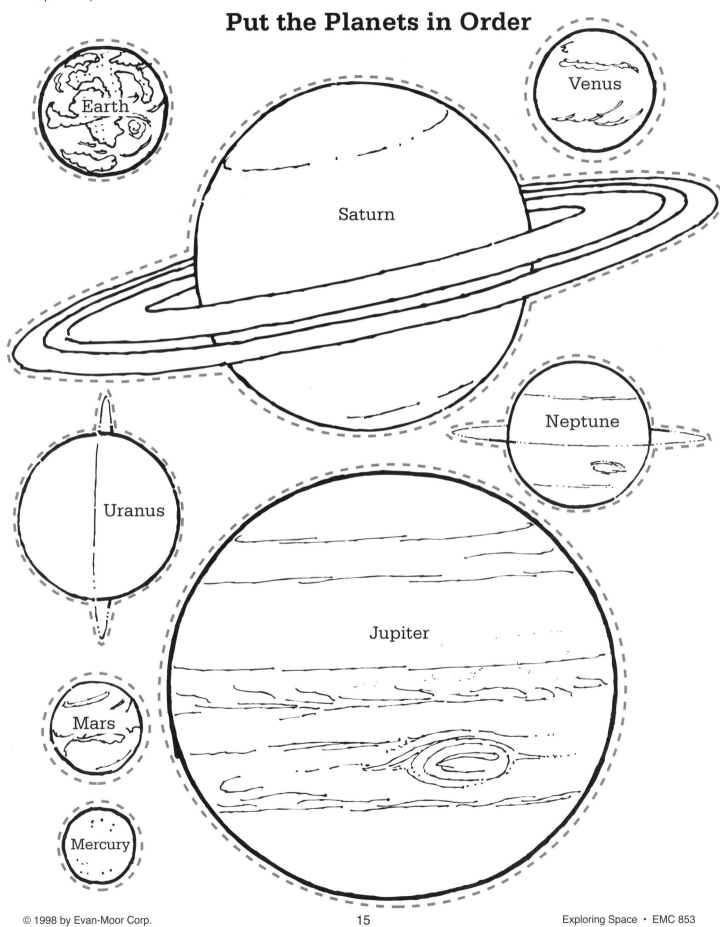

 Exploring Space • EMC 853

Stars are huge balls of hot, glowing gases.

Wondering About Stars

- Recite "Twinkle, Twinkle, Little Star" with your students. Ask, "What was the writer of the poem wondering about? Have you ever wondered about stars?" Allow time for students to share what they've wondered.
- Begin a KWL chart on stars.

1. Divide a large sheet of butcher paper into three columns and title it as shown.
2. List the things your students know about stars in the first column. Some of this may be misinformation. Leave it for now; you will cross it out as students learn more.
3. List questions students want answered in the second column. As the unit progresses, add new questions that arise.
4. Write in the last column as questions are answered. Include any other information students learn.

Stars

What We Know	What We Want to Find Out	What We Learned
Stars are in the sky.	What are stars made of?	
Stars are far away.	Why do stars twinkle?	
We see stars at night.	Are all stars alike?	
	Why are stars so little?	

Gathering Information

- Read books such as *How Far Is a Star?* by Sidney Rosen (Lerner Publishing Group, 1992), *Do Stars Have Points?* by Melvin Berger & Gilda Berger (Scholastic Inc., 1998), and *Seeing Stars* by James Muridan (Candlewick Press, 1998).

- Record information learned in the class logbook on a page entitled "Stars."

Stars

Stars are made of hot gases.

Stars are very far away.

We see stars at night.

 Exploring Space • EMC 853

What Is a Star?

Use a candle to model a star.

1. Have students sit in a circle around a candle. Turn out the lights. Have students tell what they see. Light the candle. Now have them tell what they can see. Have them describe the light source. *(The candle is burning. It makes light.)*

2. Place your hand close enough to the candle flame to feel the heat. Ask, "What am I feeling when I do this?" *(It is hot.)* Ask students to explain where the heat is coming from. *(It is hot when things burn. The burning candle makes heat.)*

3. Have students explain how the candle is like what happens with a star. *(Stars are burning and they make light.)* You may have to explain that stars also give off heat but, except for our sun, the stars are too far away for us to feel it. Add any new information to the class logbook.

Remind students not to use candles and matches without adult supervision.

Stars Minibook

- Reproduce the minibook on pages 18–20 for each student. Read and complete the book together.

- Make additions and corrections to the class logbook. Use copies of page 4 for students to write about stars for their individual logbooks.

Stars

There are billions of stars in the sky. Stars are so far away from Earth that we see them as twinkling dots of light. You can see about 2,000 stars using just your eyes. You can see more with binoculars or a telescope.

1

Stars are huge balls of hot gases. Stars use the gases to make heat and light. Most stars are so far away that we cannot feel the heat.

2

The stars we see when we look up at the sky belong to a group of stars called "the Milky Way."

Can you guess why?

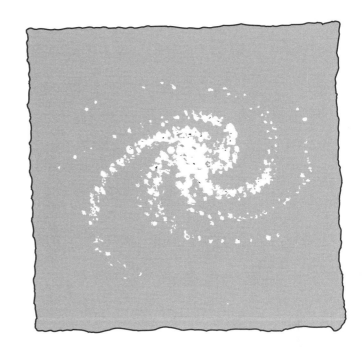

_____

_____

_____

_____

3

Match:

1. A star is

2. Stars are

3. A star makes

4. The stars in our sky are

• heat and light.

• part of the Milky Way.

• a ball of hot gases.

• very far away.

4

Why do stars twinkle? Light comes from the stars in straight lines. When the light gets to Earth, it must pass through layers of air that are around the Earth (**atmosphere**). The air makes the light bend. When you see stars twinkling, it's really light from the stars bending as it goes through the air.

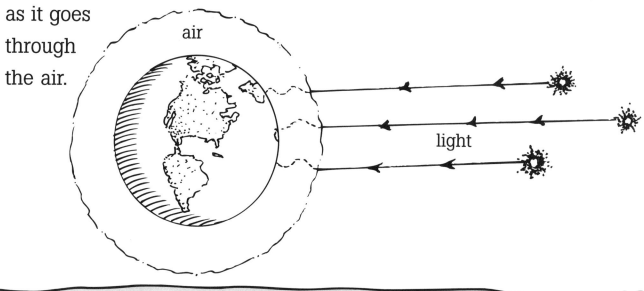

Connect the dots to make a star.

Our sun is a star.

Is Our Sun a Star?

• Ask students to give reasons why our sun is a star or why it is not. Then read books such as *I Can Read about the Sun and Other Stars* by Richard Harris (Troll Communications,1996); *The Sun, Our Nearest Star* by Franklyn M. Branley (Thomas Y. Crowell, 1988,); and *Can You Catch a Falling Star?* by Sidney Rosen (Carolrhoda Books, 1995).

• Have students recall what they learned from the books. Ask questions such as these to clarify information:

> "If our sun is a star, why can we see it during the day?"
> "Is our sun the largest star in the galaxy?"
> "Could people live on the sun? Explain your answer."
> "Why shouldn't we look at the sun?"

• Record information learned on a class logbook page entitled "Our Sun."

Our Sun

The sun is a star.

We see it in the daytime.

The sun makes light.

The sun makes heat.

Why Do We Need the Sun?

• Review the sun's characteristics (It makes light and heat.) Ask, "Why is this important to the Earth?" Use guided questioning to help students reach these understandings:

> –plants need light to make food for themselves
> –people and animals need plants for their food
> –without the heat from the sun, Earth would be
>   too cold for people, plants, and animals to live

• Reproduce page 23 for each student. They are to list three reasons the sun is important to us.

Our Sun Minibook

- Reproduce pages 24 and 25 for each student. Read and complete the pages together.
- Make corrections and additions to the class logbook page entitled "Our Sun."

Extension Activity—Eclipse of the Sun

- Read *Eclipse—Darkness in Daytime* by Franklyn M. Branley (HarperCollins, 1988). After reading, ask, "What happens to the sun during an eclipse? How does this happen?"
- Use the following activity to model an eclipse:

1. Select students to hold the items representing the sun (lamp), Earth (globe), and moon (soccer ball or volleyball). Position them as shown in the illustration.
2. The Earth and the sun remain still as the moon orbits the Earth. The person representing the Earth will see the eclipse as the moon passes directly in front of the sun.
3. Repeat with other students taking turns holding the globe and watching as the "moon" passes and causes an "eclipse."

Note: Caution students not to look directly at the light bulb or touch it.

Note: Reproduce this page for each student to use with page 21.

Name____

Why We Need the Sun

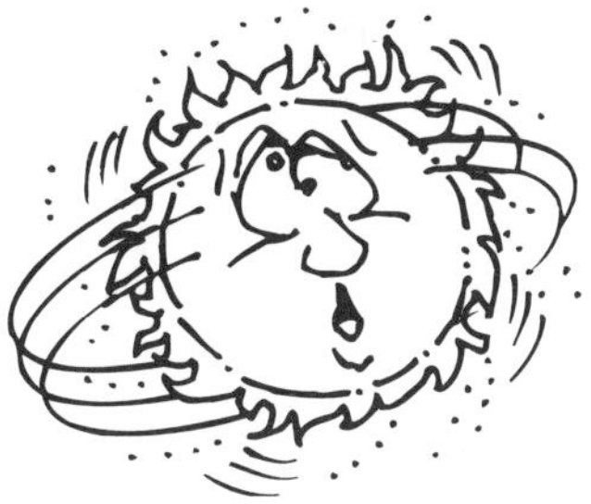

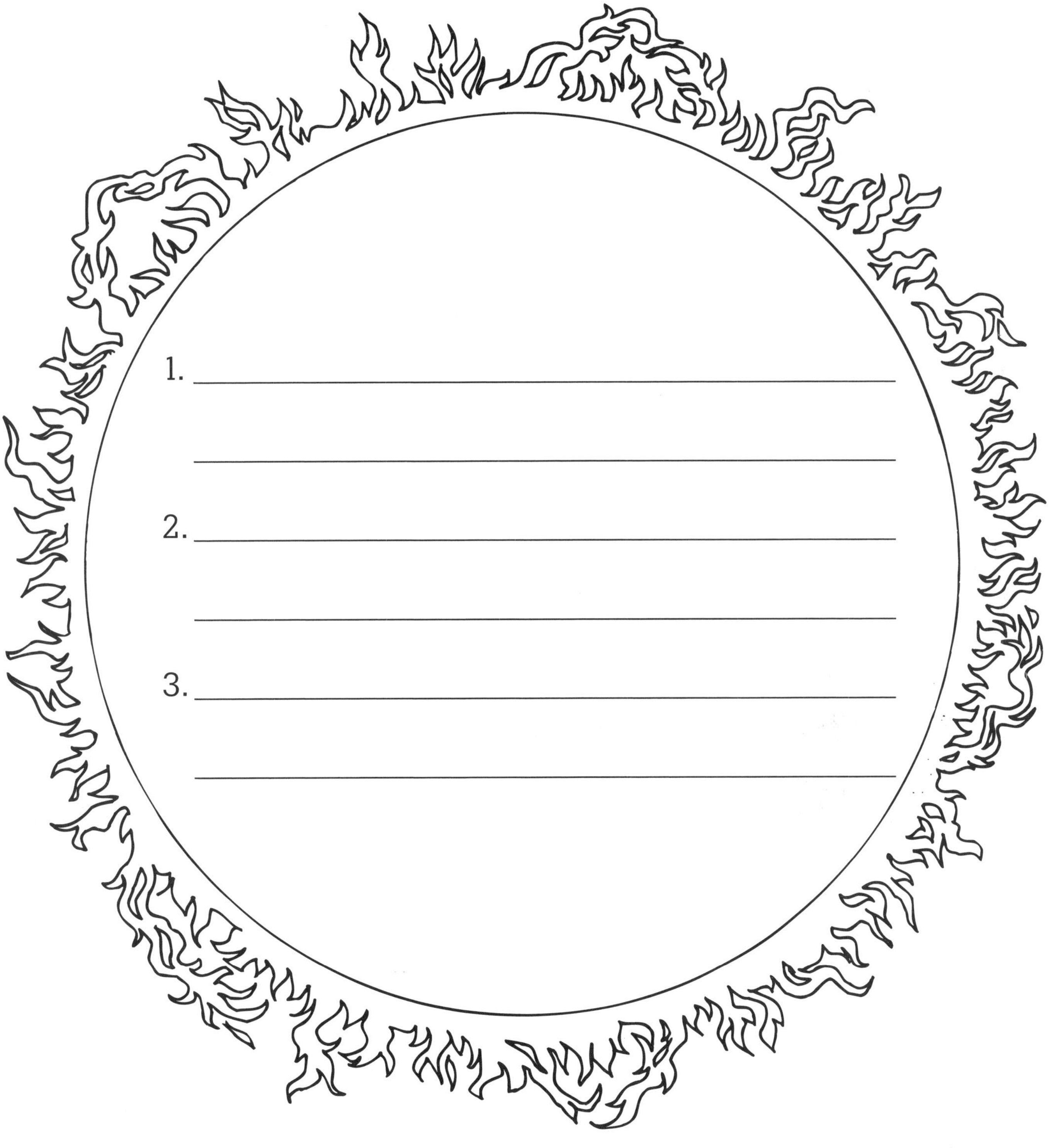

1. ____

____

2. ____

____

3. ____

____

Name_____

Our Sun

Our sun is a star. It is the star we know best because we see it almost every day. The sun is much bigger than Earth. It looks small because it is so far away (93 million miles or 150 million kilometers).

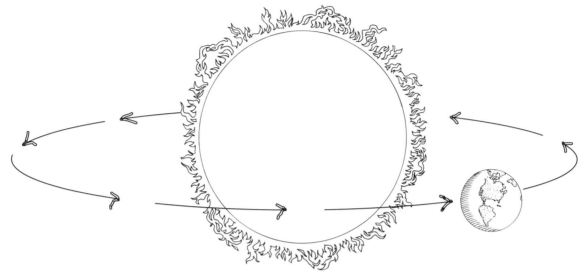

The Earth travels around the sun. This trip takes one year.

1

- -

Why can we see the sun but seldom see other stars during the day? Stars are always in the sky. Our sun makes so much light, it hides the other stars in the daytime. At night, when the sun is not in our part of the sky, we can see the other stars.

2

The sun gives off energy. A small part of the sun's energy travels to Earth. It gives us heat and light. Without the energy of sunlight, the Earth would be frozen and lifeless.

Plants need the sunlight, too. It helps plants make food for us to eat and oxygen for us to breathe.

Circle the things that need sunlight.

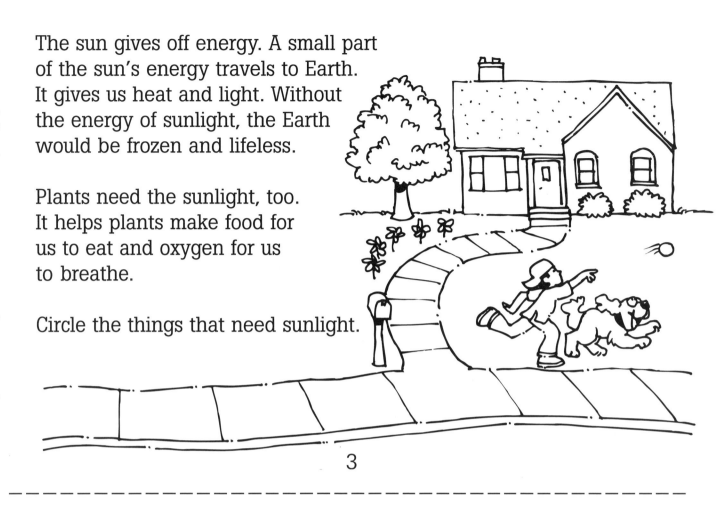

3

Fill in the blanks:

1. The sun gives us _____ and _____.

2. Plants need sunlight to make _____ and _____.

3. Without the sun, the Earth would _____

_____.

4

Groups of stars seen together are called constellations.

Naming Star Pictures

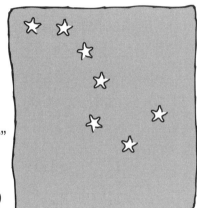

- Read *Her Seven Brothers* by Paul Gobel (Simon & Schuster, 1988). Use guided questioning to help students understand how people have tried to explain what they see in the sky.

  "Did people always know as much about the stars as we do?"
  "Why do you think people made up stories about the stars?
  "Do you see pictures when you look at the stars?"
  "Can anyone tell me the word scientists use for these star pictures?"
  Provide the term "constellation" if no one mentions it.

- Then read *The Big Dipper* by Franklyn Branley (HarperCollins, 1991) to present true facts about the constellation.

- Make overhead transparencies of pages 28 and 29. Cut the pictures on page 29 along the lines. Point to one of the star arrangements on the overlay. Ask students to describe what it looks like to them. Then lay the picture over the constellation as you give the name for the constellation.

Make a Star Box

Materials

- shoe box
- black paper
- flashlight
- pencil
- cellophane tape

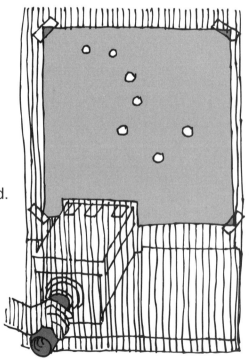

Steps to Follow

1. Leave the cover on the box. Remove one end of the box. Cut an opening the size of the flashlight in the opposite end.
2. Cut cards the same size as the open end of the box from black paper. Make one constellation on each card.
   a. First draw points to represent the stars.
   b. Then punch a hole on each of the points using a sharp nail or thick pin. Try to keep the holes round.
3. Hold or tape a constellation card over the open end of the box. Place the flashlight through the box opening.
4. Close the curtains. Turn off the classroom lights. Point the box at a wall or chalkboard. Turn on the flashlight. Enjoy your star pictures.

Exploring Space • EMC 853

Constellation Minibook

- Reproduce page 30 for each student. They are to fold the book together along the lines. Read and complete the pages together.

Star Pictures

Some bunches of stars look like pictures in the sky.

Scientists call the pictures constellations.

The Big Dipper is a constellation.

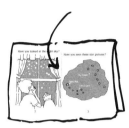

- Write a page entitled "Star Pictures" for the class logbook. Provide each student with a copy of page 4. Have them write about constellations for their individual logbooks.

The North Star and the Big Dipper

- Explain that long ago sailors and other travelers looked for the North Star to guide them. Read *Follow the Drinking Gourd* by Rabbit (Macmillan Publishing, 1997). Ask students to describe how the North Star helped the people in the story.

Say, "In *Follow the Drinking Gourd,* the Big Dipper helped people find the North Star. The two stars that make the front of the dipper are called the Pointers. If you follow a straight line out from the Pointers, you will come to the North Star. The Big Dipper changes position in the sky, but the North Star is always in the same place."

- Make the wheel on page 31 to observe the relationship between the positions of the North Star and the Big Dipper. Each student will need a copy of the pattern, a 9" (23 cm) square of blue construction paper with an X marked in the center, a paper fastener, crayons, and scissors.

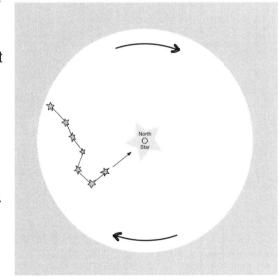

Find the Big Dipper

Reproduce the homework activity on page 32. Students are to look up at the night sky and try to locate the Big Dipper. When the forms are returned, have students explain what they did to find the constellation. Help students who were unable to find it figure out the reason. *(It wasn't a clear enough night; the neighborhood was too light to see many stars; etc.)*

Constellations

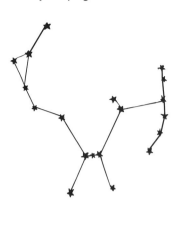

❶ The Fish (Pisces)

❷ The Hunter (Orion)

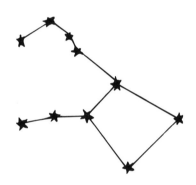

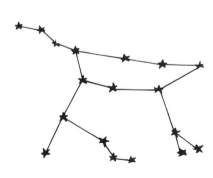

❸ The Winged Horse (Pegasus)

❹ The Lion (Leo)

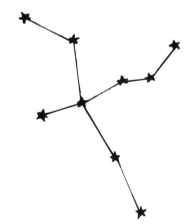

❺ The Swan (Cygnus)

❻ The Great Bear (Ursa Major)

1 The Fish (Pisces)

2 The Hunter (Orion)

3 The Winged Horse (Pegasus)

4 The Lion (Leo)

5 The Swan (Cygnus)

6 The Great Bear (Ursa Major)

Name
_____

Star Picture

Long ago men gave names to groups of stars. These groups are called constellations.

fold 1

fold 2

Exploring Space • EMC 853

1

Have you looked at the night sky?

2

Have you seen these star pictures?

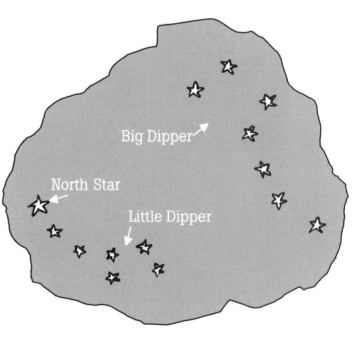

Big Dipper

North Star

Little Dipper

3

Connect the dots to see the constellation hidden here.

Circle the name of this constellation.

Draco (dragon)
Big Dipper
Orion (the hunter)

4

Where Is the North Star?

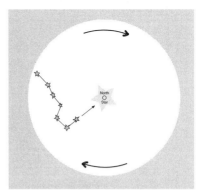

1. Color the North Star and the stars in the Big Dipper.
2. Cut out the North Star and the circle.
3. Push the paper fastener through
   the North Star
   the small circle in the center of the wheel
   the X in the middle of the blue paper

Turn the circle and watch the Big Dipper constellation move around the North Star. Watch how the Big Dipper changes.

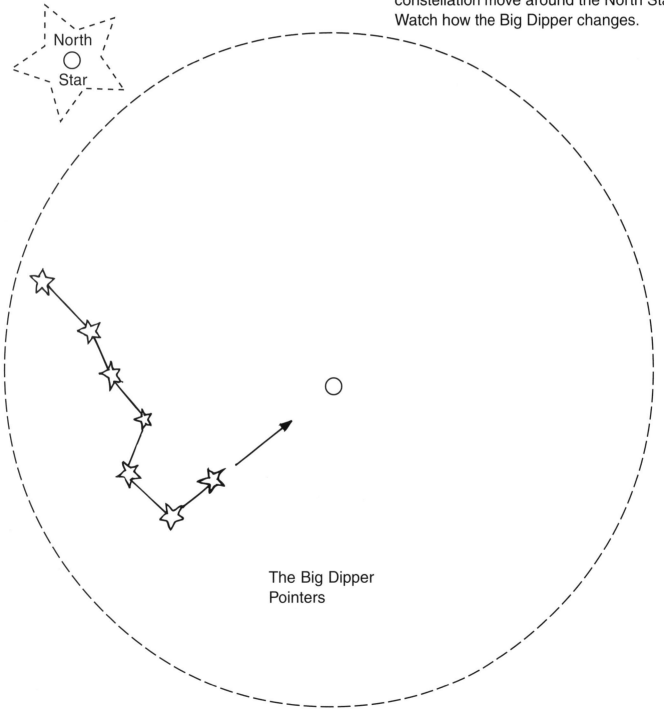

North
○
Star

The Big Dipper
Pointers

Dear Parents,

We are learning about star pictures (constellations) as part of our study of the stars. Please accompany your child outside on a clear night to look for the Big Dipper constellation. He or she is to complete the form and return it to school by _____ .
date

Thank you for your help.

Sincerely,

- -

Name_____

Look for the Big Dipper.
It might look like this:

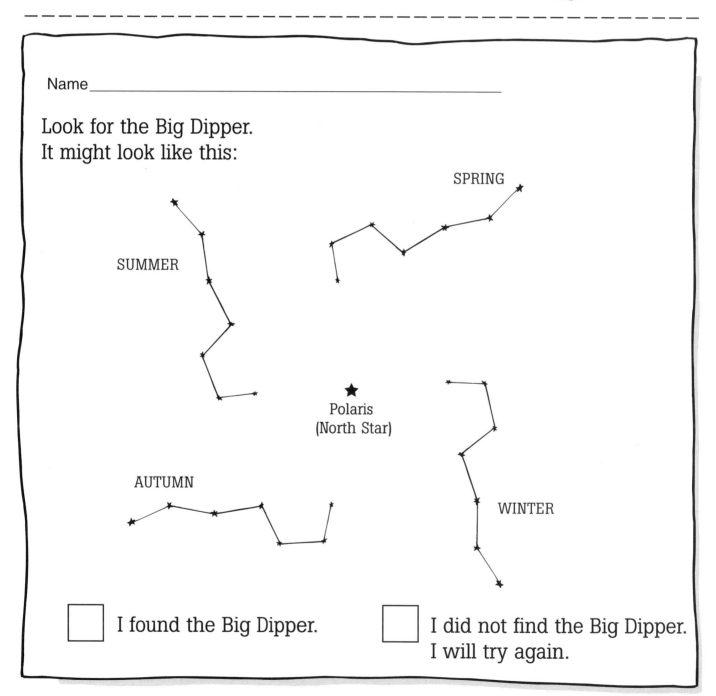

SPRING

SUMMER

Polaris
(North Star)

AUTUMN

WINTER

☐ I found the Big Dipper.   ☐ I did not find the Big Dipper.
I will try again.

     Exploring Space • EMC 853

Each planet in our solar system has unique characteristics.

What We Know About Planets

- Engage students in a discussion to see how much they already know about the planets in our solar system. Record what they recall on a page entitled "Planets" for the class logbook. You will return to this page later to make additions and corrections.

- Explain that the students are going to become "space travelers," exploring the planets in our solar system. Before beginning, ask students to recall the names of all eight planets. Add these to the "Planets" logbook page.

Across the Solar System

- Prepare a chart entitled "The Planets" on a large sheet of butcher paper. Divide the chart into eight sections. Label each section with the name of one planet.

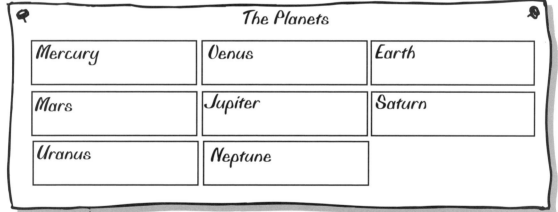

The Planets

Mercury	Venus	Earth
Mars	Jupiter	Saturn
Uranus	Neptune	

- Choose an up-to-date book on the solar system that describes each of the eight planets. Read each description aloud, and then have students describe the planet. Record this information in the correct box on the chart. Add new information to the chart as it is gathered.

- Write a definition of "planet" for the class logbook. Provide copies of page 4 for each student. Have them copy the definition for their individual logbooks.

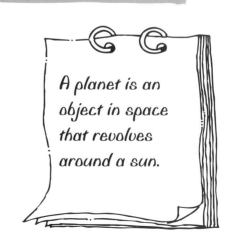

A planet is an object in space that revolves around a sun.

Exploring Space • EMC 853

Gather More Information

The following sources can help students review basic information and acquire new information to add to the chart begun on page 33.

1. Show a video or filmstrip about the planets.

2. Visit approved sites on the World Wide Web.

The Planets Minibook

Reproduce pages 37–41 for each student. Read and discuss the minibook together. This can be done in one sitting or you can read about one planet at a time.

Note: Planets' distances from the sun are rounded to the nearest million miles.

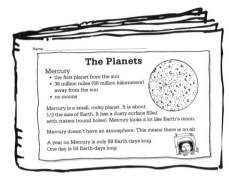

Assess Understanding

Reproduce pages 42–50 for each student. Bind the pages together into a book or add them to each student's logbook.

Students use the information from the "Planets" chart, the minibook, and what they learn from other sources to complete the forms. They are to color each planet, and then write three facts about it. Then they are to design an imaginary planet and describe it using characteristics that planets have. For example, they may list how many moons it has or how far it is from the sun.

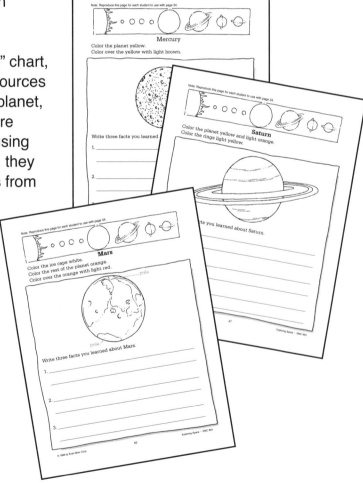

Exploring Space • EMC 853

Orbiting the Sun

The planets take different amounts of time to go around the sun. This activity helps students understand why this happens.

1. Make a large yellow sun from butcher paper. Enlarge a picture of each planet (Use any of the pictures provided in this unit.) Assign "parts" to students. Tell remaining students that they are astronomers studying the planets.

2. Take the class outside. Have the "sun" stand in the center of the playground. Place the "planets" with their pictures in the correct order from the sun with "Neptune" being near the edge of the playing area. Have the "planets" walk around the sun. Remind students that they are revolving around the sun.

3. Ask the "astronomers" to explain what they saw. *(It took some planets much longer to go around the sun than the others.)* Have them explain why this is true. *(Some planets had to go farther than others.)* Ask, "Which planet has the shortest trip? Which planet has the longest trip?" Explain that the amount of time it takes each planet to revolve around the sun is called a year. Ask, "Is a year the same amount of time on Venus as on Neptune?"

4. Have students record what they learned for their individual logbooks, using the form on page 5.

How Far?

Make a model to show the relative distances of the planets from the sun. You will need a display area at least eight feet (two and one-half meters) long.

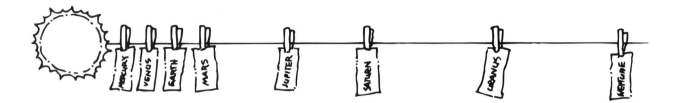

Materials

- 12" (30.5 cm) square of yellow construction paper
- eight 1" x 6" (2.5 x 15 cm) pieces of tagboard
- 8 clothespins
- 8' (2.5 meters) piece of roving or thin clothesline
- ruler
- measuring tape

Steps to Follow

1. Have a student cut a large sun out of the yellow paper. Attach the sun to one end of the display area.
2. Pin the roving or clothesline from the sun to the end of the display area.
3. Give each of eight students a 1" x 6" (2.5 x 15 cm) piece of tagboard. Have each student write the name of a different planet on the tag.
4. Using the following measurements, pin each planet to the line with a clothespin. (Have students help with the measurements as much as possible.)

Distance from the sun:

Planet		
Mercury	1"	(2.5 cm)
Venus	1 1/2"	(3.8 cm)
Earth	2"	(5 cm)
Mars	3"	(7.6 cm)
Jupiter	11 1/2"	(29.2 cm)
Saturn	19"	(48.3 cm)
Uranus	38"	(96.5 cm)
Neptune	60"	(152.4 cm)

Follow Up

When the model is complete, ask questions such as:

"Which planet is closest to and which is farthest from the sun?"

"Which planets are closer to the sun than Earth? Farther away?"

"If you travel from Earth, which planet would be closest to visit?"

"Which trip would be longer—Jupiter to Uranus or Mars to Saturn?"

Exploring Space • EMC 853

The Planets

Mercury

- the first planet from the sun
- 36 million miles (58 million kilometers)
  away from the sun
- no moons

Mercury is a small, rocky planet. It is about
1/3 the size of Earth. It has a dusty surface filled
with **craters** (round holes). Mercury looks a lot like Earth's moon.

Mercury doesn't have an atmosphere. This means there is no air.

A year on Mercury is only 88 Earth-days long.
One day is 59 Earth-days long.

1

Exploring Space • EMC 853

Venus

- the second planet from the sun
- 67 million miles (108 million kilometers)
  away from the sun
- no moons

You can find Venus shining low in the
western sky at night. It is the brightest
object except for the moon.

Venus is almost the same size as Earth. It is a dry, hot planet with tall
mountains and deep valleys. Venus is covered in thick, yellow clouds.
Strong winds blow the clouds around.

A year on Venus is 225 Earth-days long.
One day is 243 Earth-days long.

2

Earth

- the third planet from the sun
- 93 million miles (149 million kilometers) from the sun
- one moon

The Earth is a ball of rock almost covered by oceans. It is not too hot and not too cold. As far as we know, it is the only planet with air we can breathe. It is the only planet with plants and animals. It is just right for us to live.

From space Earth looks like a ball covered with white clouds. Under the clouds are brown land areas and blue oceans.

A year on Earth is 365 days long.
One day is 24 hours long.

Mars

- the fourth planet from the sun
- 141 million miles (227 million kilometers} from the sun
- 2 moons

Mars is about half the size of Earth. It is a desert except for the ice caps at the north and south poles. It has tall mountains and deep canyons. The soil is full of rust-colored iron dust. This makes Mars look red. Strong winds blow up big storms of the red dust. It is very cold on Mars. Mars doesn't have an atmosphere.

A year on Mars is 687 Earth-days long.
One day is 24 1/2 Earth-hours long.

Jupiter
- the fifth planet from the sun
- 483 million miles (778 million kilometers) from the sun
- 63 known moons

Jupiter is the largest planet in the solar system. If Jupiter were hollow, more than 1,000 planets the size of Earth could fit inside it.

Jupiter is a giant ball of gas with a small rocky center. It is covered by thick clouds. It is freezing cold at the top of the clouds. It is boiling hot at the center of Jupiter. There is a large red spot on Jupiter that may be a giant storm. A thin ring of rocks orbits the planet.

A year on Jupiter is 12 Earth-years long.
One day is about 10 Earth-hours long.

5

Saturn
- the sixth planet from the sun
- 887 million miles (1 billion, 416 million kilometers) from the sun
- at least 56 moons

Like Jupiter, Saturn is a giant ball of gas with a rocky center. It is the second largest planet. It is about 10 times as large as Earth.

Many rings orbit the planet. The rings are made of bits of ice and rock. Clouds cover the planet. Saturn is freezing cold at the top of the clouds. It is very hot at its center.

A year on Saturn is about 30 Earth-years long.
One day is only 10 1/2 Earth-hours long.

6

Uranus

- the seventh planet from the sun
- 1 billion, 783 million miles (2 billion, 870 million kilometers) from the sun
- 27 moons

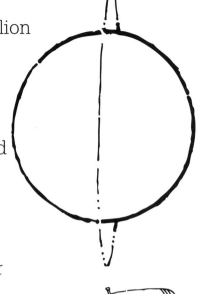

Uranus, too, is a giant gas ball with a rocky center. It has some rings. The rings are thin and dark. Uranus looks blue-green. A thick haze covers the planet. Uranus is so far from the sun that it is very, very cold.

Uranus rotates in a different way than the other planets. It tilts over on its side.

A year on Uranus is 84 Earth-years long.
One day is 17 Earth-hours long.

Neptune

- the eighth planet from the sun
- 2 billion, 794 million miles (4 billion, 497 million kilometers) from the sun
- at least 13 moons

Neptune is a large blue-green ball of gas with a center of rock and iron. Neptune has faint rings. The planet is covered with clouds. Neptune has high winds and many storms. Because Neptune is so far from the sun, it is very, very cold.

A year on Neptune is 165 Earth-years long.
One day is about 16 Earth-hours long.

Planet Patrol

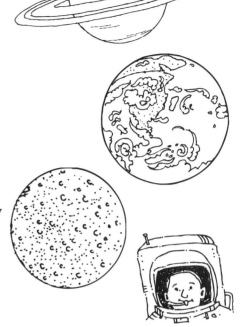

Which planet do you think is…

1. the hottest?
   a. Mercury   b. Venus   c. Mars

2. the lightest in weight?
   a. Saturn   b. Mars   c. Earth

3. the windiest?
   a. Uranus   b. Neptune   c. Saturn

4. the fastest?
   a. Earth   b. Jupiter   c. Mercury

5. the brightest?
   a. Venus   b. Pluto   c. Mars

Answers on the next page.

9

Answers to Planet Patrol

1. **b. Venus.** Mercury is closer to the sun but Venus has thicker air. Thicker air traps heat better than thinner air. The temperature of Venus is hotter than boiling water.

2. **a. Saturn.** It's even lighter than the smallest planet, Mercury. Saturn is made up of gases. Gases are the lightest matter. So even though Saturn is the second-largest planet, it is still the lightest.

3. **b. Neptune.** Winds blow up to 1,200 miles per hour (2,000 kilometers per hour) on Neptune. How fast is that? A car on the highway goes about 60 miles per hour (97 kilometers per hour).

4. **c. Mercury.** Mercury travels around the sun faster than any other planet. That's because it is the closest planet to the sun. It travels less distance.

5. **a. Venus.** Only the Earth's moon is brighter in the night sky than Venus. The best time to see Venus in the sky is early in the morning or early in the evening.

10

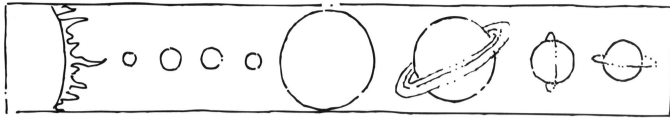

Mercury

Color the planet yellow.

Color over the yellow with light brown.

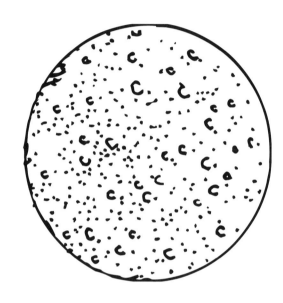

Write three facts you learned about Mercury.

1. _____

_____

2. _____

_____

3. _____

_____

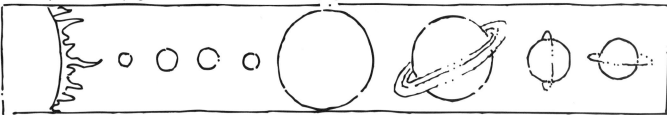

Venus

Color the planet yellow.

Color over the yellow with light brown.

Write three facts you learned about Venus.

1. _____

_____

2. _____

_____

3. _____

_____

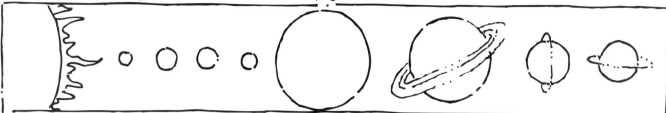

Earth

Color the planet.

land — brown   **water** — blue   **clouds** — white

Write three facts you learned about Earth.

1. _____

_____

2. _____

_____

3. _____

_____

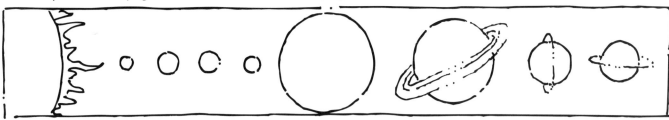

Mars

Color the ice caps white.

Color the rest of the planet orange.

Color over the orange with light red.

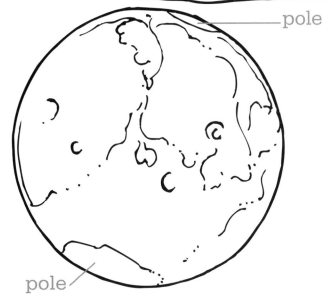

pole

pole

Write three facts you learned about Mars.

1. _____

_____

2. _____

_____

3. _____

_____

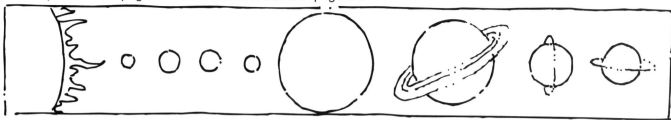

Jupiter

Color the planet orange, yellow, red, and light brown.
Make the Great Red Spot dark red.

Write three facts you learned about Jupiter.

1. _____

_____

2. _____

_____

3. _____

_____

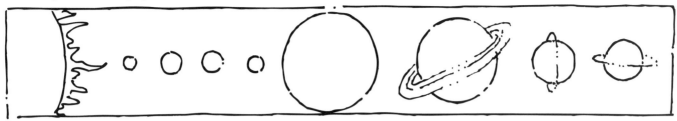

Saturn

Color the planet yellow and light orange.
Color the rings light yellow.

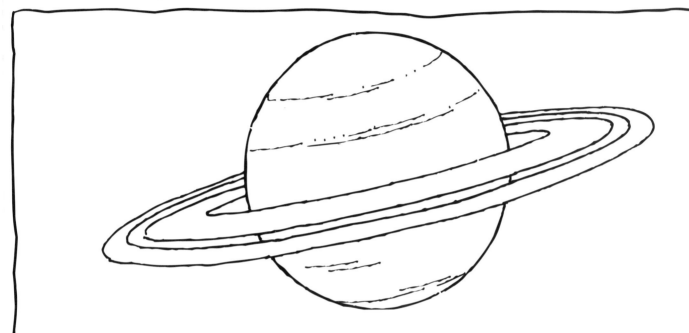

Write three facts you learned about Saturn.

1. _____

_____

2. _____

_____

_____

3. _____

_____

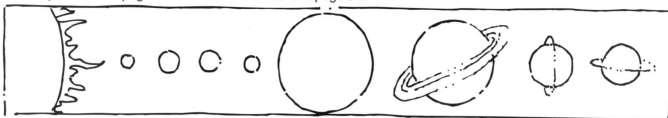

Uranus

Color the planet blue-green.

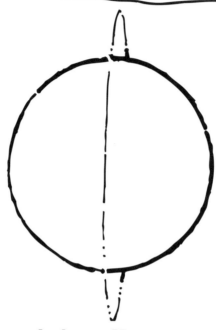

Write three facts you learned about Uranus.

1. _____

_____

2. _____

_____

3. _____

_____

 Exploring Space • EMC 853

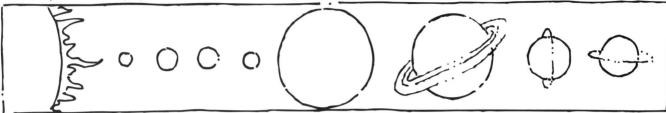

Color the planet blue.   **Neptune**
Color the clouds white.
Make the Great Dark Spot dark blue.

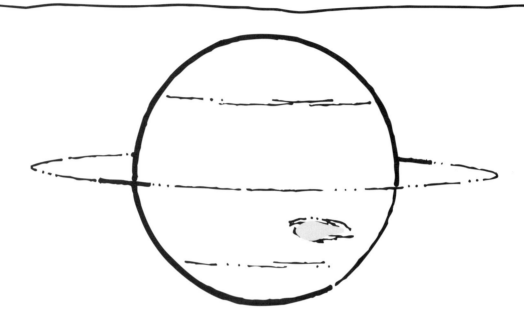

Write three facts you learned about Neptune.

1. _____

   _____

2. _____

   _____

3. _____

   _____

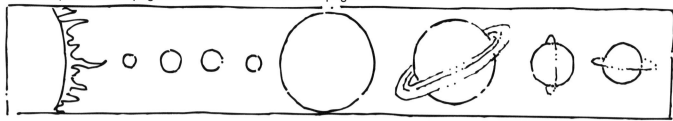

My Own Planet

Imagine you are a space scientist. You find a new planet. Draw your planet in the box below. Give it a name. Then color it.

Tell three things about your planet.

1. _____

_____

2. _____

_____

3. _____

_____

The Earth has one satellite called the moon.

Moons

- Generate interest in moons by asking students to answer a riddle about Earth's moon. Give the clues one at a time, calling on a student to try to give an answer after each clue. Continue giving clues until you receive the answer "moon."

  "This object is part of the solar system."

  "It is smaller than Earth."

  "It is usually seen at night."

  "It has holes called craters on its surface."

  "It goes around the Earth."

  "It seems to change shape on different nights."

  "If you look up at night, you will probably see it."

  Explain that most planets have one or more moons. These moons are also called satellites.

- Read one or more books such as *The Moon* by Gail Gibbons (Holiday House, 1997) or *What the Moon Is Like* by Franklyn M. Branley (HarperCollins, 1986).

- Ask students to recall information from the material read. Write about the moon on a class logbook page entitled "Moon." Use copies of page 4 for students to write about the moon for their individual logbooks.

Moon

We see the moon at night.

The moon looks like it changes.

The moon goes around the Earth.

Its trip takes one month.

Some planets have more than one moon.

Some planets don't have any moons.

How Are Moon Craters Made?

Ask students how the craters on the moon are made. Provide the information if students do not know. (Big rocks from space hit the moon, leaving holes.)

Do the following demonstration with student assistance to simulate these occurrences.

Materials

- soft soil or sand
- shallow pan
- several rocks of different sizes
- page 5, reproduced for each student

Steps to Follow

1. Put the soil or sand in the pan.
2. Hold a rock over the pan (about as high as your chin).
3. Drop the rock.
4. Lift it out carefully so you do not change the shape of the crater. Repeat with different-sized rocks, smoothing the sand before each try.
5. Then repeat holding the rocks at different heights.
6. Record discoveries. (Students describe what they did, what they saw, and what they learned.)

Follow Up

Have students explain what they discovered about craters. *(Both rock size and the height from which it is dropped affect the size and depth of the crater.)* Explain that some craters were created long ago during a time when the moon had active volcanoes.

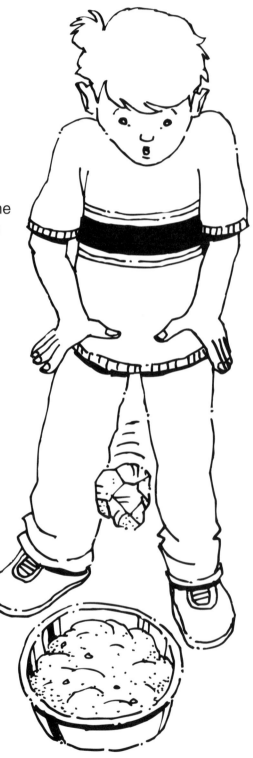

What Is the Source of the Moon's Light?

Ask students to think about this question as you do the following demonstration with student assistance. Explain that the mirror represents the moon and the flashlight represents the sun.

Materials

- mirror
- flashlight
- logbook form on page 5, reproduced for each student

Steps to Follow

1. Shut the curtains and turn off the lights.
2. Turn on the flashlight. Point it at a wall. Observe what happens to the light.
3. Point the flashlight at the mirror. Observe what happens to the light.
4. Record what you observe.

Follow Up

Ask students to describe what they saw. *(When the flashlight pointed at the wall, we just saw the wall. When the flashlight pointed at the mirror, the light bounced off, and we could see other things in the classroom.)*

Explain that this is called reflected light. The sunlight shines on the moon just like the flashlight shone on the mirror. The sunlight is reflected away from the moon just as the light was reflected off the mirror. Neither the mirror nor the moon produce light. They both reflect light.

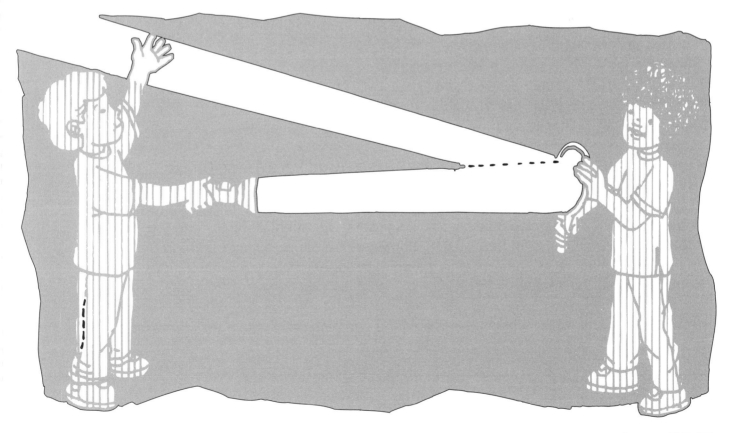

Phases of the Moon

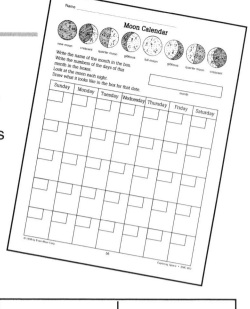

- Reproduce the moon calendar on page 56 and the parent letter on page 57 for each student. Students are to observe and record the changes they see in the moon over the period of one month.

  When the calendars are returned to class, discuss what students observed. Ask questions to help them explain what they saw.
  "Did the moon look the same every night?"
  "What kinds of changes did you see?"
  "How does this happen?"

- Use the following activity to help students understand what was occurring as they observed the changes in the moon. It is important they understand that the moon remains a sphere. It appears to change shape because we see the lighted portion from different angles.

  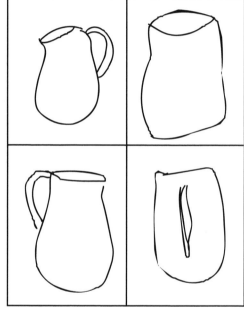

  1. Each student needs a sheet of drawing paper folded into quarters, a crayon, and a piece of cardboard to use as a drawing table.
  2. Students sit in a circle around a large object with a handle (mug, pitcher, soup tureen, etc.) and draw what they see from their angle.
  3. Have everyone move counterclockwise one quarter of the way around the circle to draw what they see from the new angle.
  4. Repeat step 2 two more times.

Have students look at their pictures and explain what has happened. *(Each time, we saw the pitcher in a different way.)*
Explain how this relates to what we see as we watch the moon change.

- Read *Where Does the Moon Go?* by Sidney Rosen (Lerner Publishing Group, 1992).

- Reproduce pages 58 and 59 for each student to use to make moon phase wheels. Each student will also need a paper fastener and scissors. Cut out both circles and the window on page 59. Put page 59 on top of page 58 and put the paper fastener through the center circles. By turning the bottom wheel to the right, the phases of the moon will appear in the correct order in the window.

Have students share their wheels with a neighbor, naming each phase as it turns up on the wheel.

　　　　　　　　　　　　　　Exploring Space • EMC 853

Moon Minibook

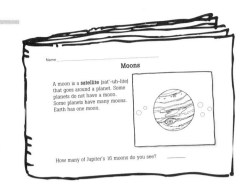

- Reproduce the moon minibook on pages 60–62 for each student. Read and complete the pages together to review what has been learned about the moon. Make changes or additions to the class and individual logbooks.

- Explain that a moon's phases are a kind of cycle. Together, write a definition of "cycle" for the class logbook.

A Lunar Eclipse

- Ask students to recall what happened during an eclipse of the sun. See if they can use that knowledge to formulate an explanation of how an eclipse of the moon happens. *(The Earth's shadow falls on the moon making it look like all or part of the moon has disappeared.)* Demonstrate a lunar eclipse with the help of students.

1. Select students to represent the sun (lamp), Earth (globe), and moon (softball or volleyball).
2. Have the "sun," "moon," and "Earth" arrange themselves with the Earth between the sun and the moon. (This has to be done carefully so that the shadow of the globe falls on the "moon." If the moon is totally in the shadow, it is a total eclipse. If part of the moon is lit, it is a partial eclipse. Have students stand by the globe to see the shadow.

- Then read *What Is an Eclipse?* by Issac Asimov (Gareth Stevens, 1991).

Space Riddles

These teacher-made flip-up riddles will help your students review the objects in our solar system.
1. Reproduce pages 63–66.
2. Color and cut out the answer circles. Glue them to construction paper squares.
3. Cut out the question circles. Place each question over the correct answer, putting glue only on the back of the tab.

Students read a question and think of the answer. They lift the flap to verify their answer.

Exploring Space • EMC 853

Moon Calendar

| new moon | crescent | quarter moon | gibbous | full moon | gibbous | quarter moon | crescent |

Write the name of the month in the box.
Write the numbers of the days of this
month in the boxes.
Look at the moon each night.
Draw what it looks like in the box for that date.

month

Sunday	Monday	Tuesday	Wednesday	Thursday	Friday	Saturday

Exploring Space • EMC 853

Dear Parents,

We are learning about the phases of the moon as part of our study of the solar system. Please help your child complete the attached moon calendar. He or she may draw a picture or write the name of the moon phase in the correct box. Leave the box blank on nights no observation was made.

Thank you for your help.

Sincerely,

Dear Parents,

We are learning about the phases of the moon as part of our study of the solar system. Please help your child complete the attached moon calendar. He or she may draw a picture or write the name of the moon phase in the correct box. Leave the box blank on nights no observation was made.

Thank you for your help.

Sincerely,

Dear Parents,

We are learning about the phases of the moon as part of our study of the solar system. Please help your child complete the attached moon calendar. He or she may draw a picture or write the name of the moon phase in the correct box. Leave the box blank on nights no observation was made.

Thank you for your help.

Sincerely,

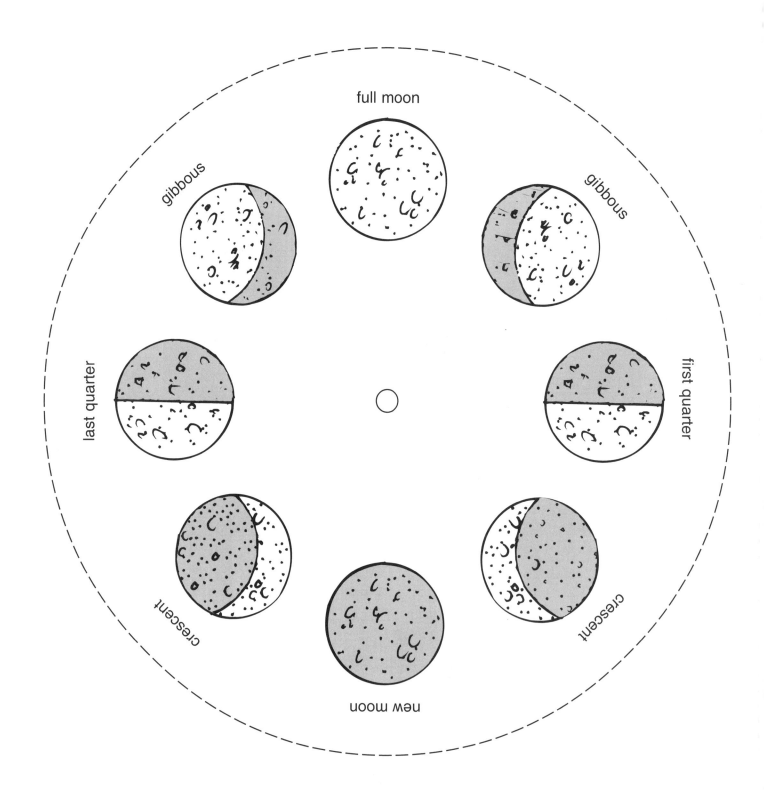

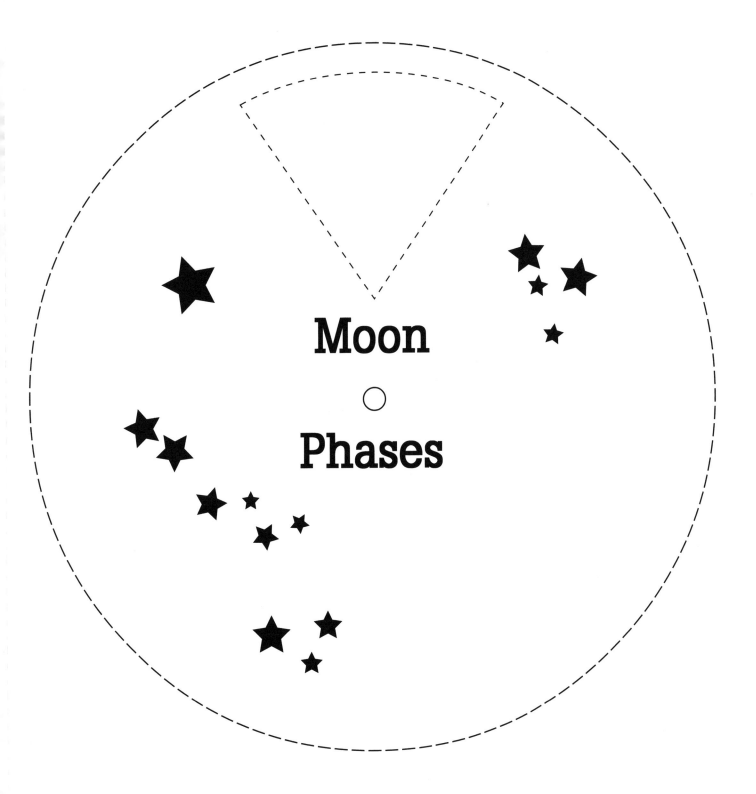

Moon
○
Phases

Moons

A moon is a **satellite** (sat'–uh–lite) that goes around a planet. Some planets do not have a moon. Some planets have many moons. Earth has one moon.

How many of Jupiter's 16 moons do you see? _____

1

Earth's Moon

The moon is our nearest neighbor in space. It is smaller than the Earth. It is smaller than the sun, too. It only looks bigger because it is much closer to the Earth. It is 240,000 miles (384,000 kilometers) away.

The moon goes around (**orbits**) the Earth one time a month (about every 29 days).

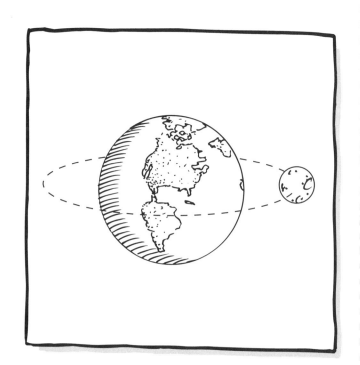

2

There is no air or water on the moon. It is dry, dusty, and lifeless. There are tall mountains and flat, dusty plains on the moon. There are many big holes called **craters** (kray'-terz). Craters are made when space rocks hit the moon.

3

The moon does not make its own light.
We can see it because it reflects light from the sun.

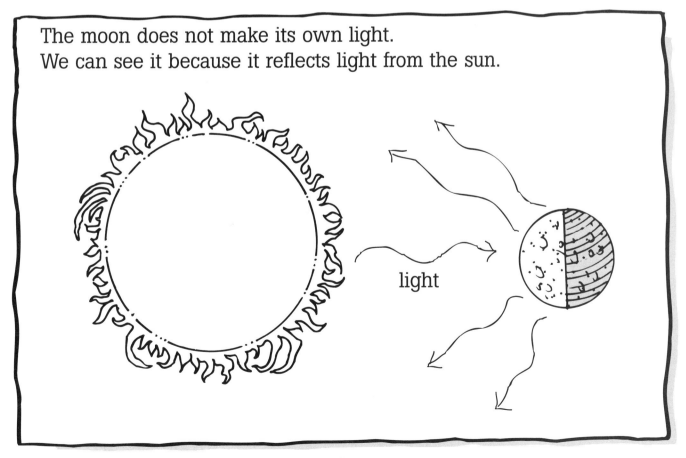

light

4

The moon turns so slowly that a day is two weeks long. Then it is night for the next two weeks.

During daytime the moon is very hot. It is hotter than boiling water. This is because there is no air to protect the moon from the hot sunlight.

At night the moon gets very cold. It is much colder than freezing. This is because there is no air to hold heat on the moon.

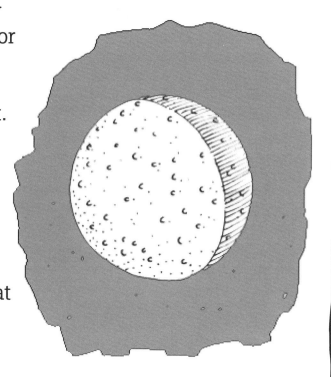

5

Men On the Moon

Twelve men have gone to the moon. They walked on the moon. They picked up rocks to bring back to Earth.

These men had to wear special suits. They had to take air to breathe. They had to take the food and water they needed for the trip.

The moon's gravity is less than on Earth. The astronauts felt lighter on the moon. They could jump higher and take longer steps, too.

Make a man on this moon. What will he be wearing?

6

Space Riddle Answer Circles

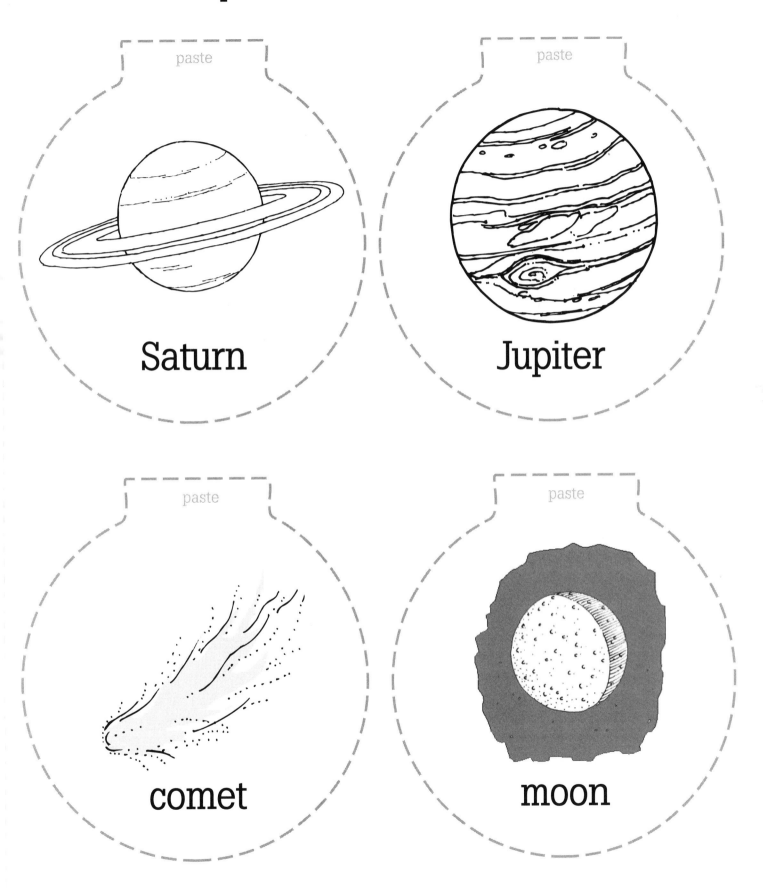

Saturn

Jupiter

comet

moon

Exploring Space • EMC 853

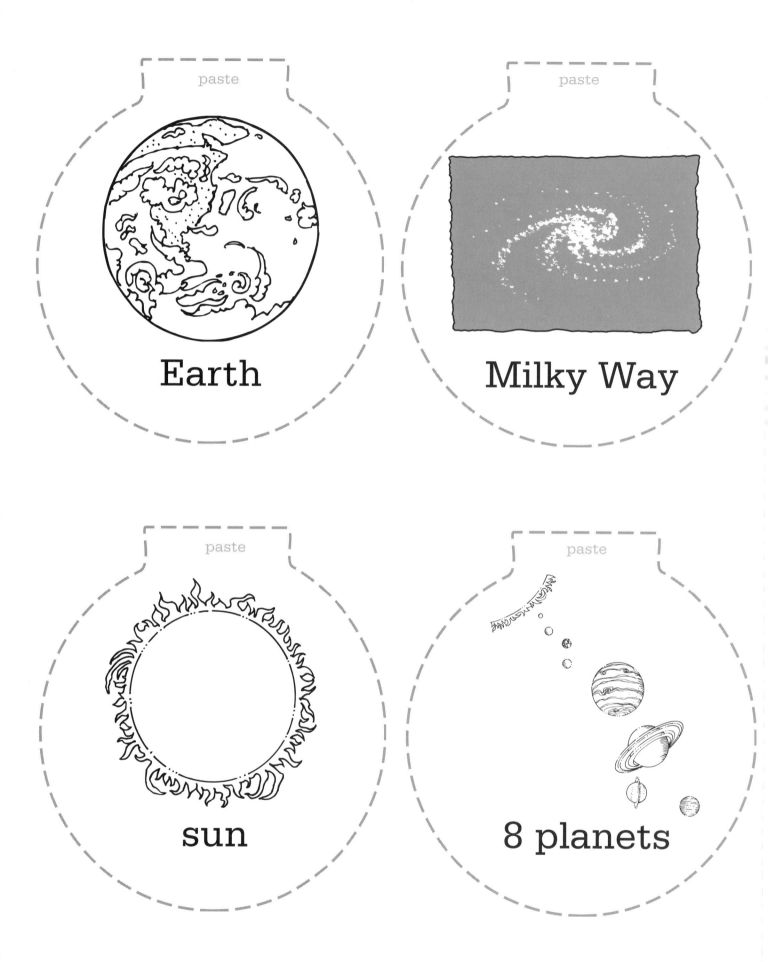

paste

Earth

paste

Milky Way

paste

sun

paste

8 planets

Exploring Space • EMC 853

Which star is closest
to the Earth?

What is the name
of our galaxy?

How many
planets
are in our solar
system?

Which planet is
almost
the same size as
Venus?

Which planet has
a Great Red Spot?

What object with a
long "tail" travels
around the solar
system?

Which planet has
the most rings?

What object that is
covered with craters
orbits the Earth?

Exploring Space • EMC 853

The Earth's movements through space cause day and night and the seasons.

How are Day and Night Different?

Engage students in a discussion of how day and night are different. List their ideas on a class logbook page entitled "Day and Night." Corrections and additions will be made later.

Sun Rise—Sun Set

As the Earth turns, the sun seems to disappear and reappear, making day and night. Help students visualize what really happens with the following demonstration.

Materials

- light source (lamp or flashlight)
- small cutout of a person (below)
- tape
- globe

Steps to Follow

1. Tape the cutout to your location on the globe.
2. Stand the globe six feet from the light source. Have the cutout facing the light source.
3. Turn out the lights. Remind students to follow the cutout on the globe.
4. Slowly rotate the globe to the right until a full circle has been made. This represents one day.
5. Rotate the globe several more times, having students say "day" and "night" as the cutout moves in and out of the light.

Follow Up

Question students about what happened.

"What did you see when the cutout was facing the light?"
(The light was shining on the cutout. It looked like daytime.)
"What did you see when the cutout turned away from the light?"
(It was in the dark. It looked like nightime.)
"What caused this to happen?"
(The globe turned. It moved the cutout around.)
"How is this like what happens to us?"
(As part of the Earth turns away from the sun it gets dark.
When it turns back to the sun it gets light again.)

Summary Activities

- Reproduce the minibook on pages 71–75. Read *What Makes Day and Night* by Franklyn Branley (HarperCollins, 1986). Then read pages 1–4 of the minibook to clarify what happens as the Earth rotates.

- Write about "Day and Night" in the class logbook. Have students use copies of page 4 to write for their individual logbooks.

Summer, Autumn, Winter, Spring

- Have students look out the class windows and describe the current season. Then ask them to describe how the weather, plants, etc., change when winter comes. Ask, "Do you know why this happens?" (You will probably get answers such as: *"The wind makes it cold in the winter. The sun isn't as warm in the winter."* Accept these answers for now. Misinformation will be cleared up as you do the activities.)

- Show a video or filmstrip or read *Why Do Seasons Change?* by Christopher Mainard (DK Publications, 1997) or *The Reasons for the Seasons* by Gail Gibbons (Holiday House, 1996).

- Ask students to share what they learned. Record this information on a page for the class logbook entitled "Seasons." Use page 4 for students to write about seasons for their individual logbooks.

What Causes Seasons to Change?

The Earth Turns on Its Axis

Bring in a toy top. Have students watch as you spin the top. Ask, "How is the top moving?" *(It turns around. It moves around on the point that sticks out.)* Point to the rod sticking out the top and bottom of the top. Explain that anything that spins moves around a center line. This is called an axis.

Explain that the Earth spins around, too. It doesn't have a pole through its center, but it does have an axis that goes from the North Pole to the South Pole. It spins around the axis.

Model this using an orange and a pencil. Push the pencil through the center of the orange to represent the axis. Spin the orange on the pencil as you say, "The Earth spins around on its axis." Show how the Earth is tipped on its axis. Ask, "Does the Earth really have a pole sticking through it? What does the Earth spin around?"

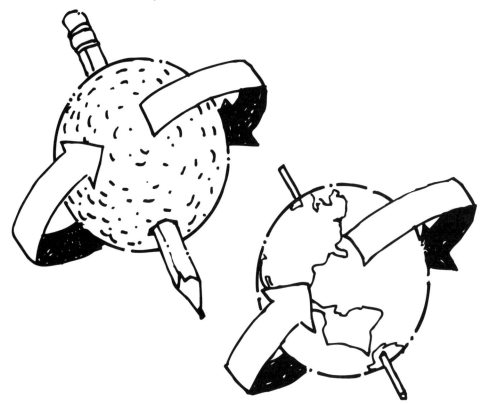

The Earth Moves around the Sun

You will need a lamp without its shade and a globe for this demonstration.

Tape the cutout of a person (page 67) on the globe approximately where you are located. Have one student hold the lamp. Another student holds the globe in the light from the lamp. Select several students to be "astronomers" studying the Earth and sun. Slowly move the globe around the lamp, always keeping it tilted in the same position. (The easiest way to do this is to keep the top of the axis pointing at an object on the wall.)

 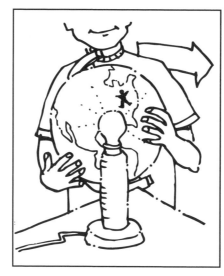 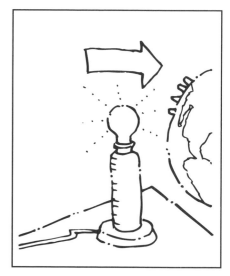

Have the observers watch to see when the North Pole is tilted toward the "sun" or away from the "sun" as you move the globe around. Explain that it is colder where you live when the axis is pointing away from the sun (winter). It is warmer when the axis is pointing toward the sun (summer). (Reverse this, tilting the South Pole, if you live in the Southern Hemisphere.)

Repeat the demonstration with new groups of students until everyone has had a chance to see the changes taking place.

Summary Activities

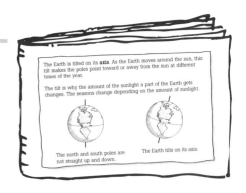

- Read pages 5–10 of the minibook "When the Earth Moves" together to further clarify what happens as the Earth revolves around the sun. Ask students to explain what they have learned.

- Make any changes or additions to the class and individual logbooks.

70

Name_____

When the Earth Moves

The Earth is always turning. It never stops.

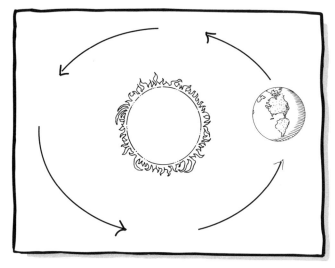

It makes one turn on its **axis** every 24 hours.

It **revolves** around the sun once every year.

1

Do you know what makes day and night?

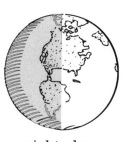

night   day   sun   day   night

The sun shines on the Earth as it spins. But sunlight shines only on the half of the Earth facing the sun. That half has day. The other half is dark. That half has night.

As the Earth spins we move from day, to night, to day, to night over and over again.

2

Does the sun move across the sky?

The sun seems to move across the sky during the day.
It is really the Earth's spinning that causes this to happen.

3

Is there day and night on the moon?

If you were on the moon, you would also have day and night. But the moon spins very slowly, so days and nights are two weeks long.

4

The Earth is tilted on its **axis**. As the Earth moves around the sun, this tilt makes the poles point toward or away from the sun at different times of the year.

The tilt is why the amount of the sunlight a part of the Earth gets changes. The seasons change depending on the amount of sunlight.

The North and South Poles are not straight up and down.

The Earth tilts on its axis.

5

When the North Pole is tilted toward the sun, the northern half of the Earth has summer. The days are long and the nights are short. The long days mean that the Earth is getting a lot of warmth from the sun.

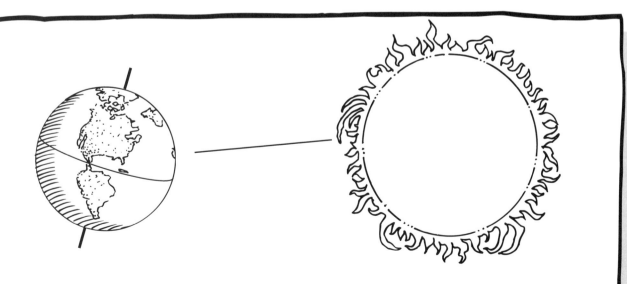

The northern half of the Earth is facing the sun. It is summer there.

6

When the North Pole is tilted away from the sun, the northern half of the Earth has winter. The days are short and the nights are long. The short days mean that the Earth is not getting much warmth from the sun.

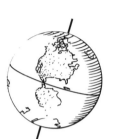

The northern half of the Earth is facing away from the sun.
It is winter there.

Spring and autumn have days and nights that are about the same length. The days are not as hot as in the summer and not as cold as in the winter.

The equator is pointing toward the sun.

The **equator** is an imaginary line around the middle of our planet. It divides the Earth in half. The seasons are opposite north and south of the equator. When it is summer to the north of the equator, it is winter to the south. When it is autumn to the south of the equator, it is spring to the north.

Match:

North of the Equator   South of the Equator

When it is summer here,   it is summer here.
When it is autumn here,   it is autumn here.
When it is winter here,   it is winter here.
When it is spring here,   it is spring here.

9

Are the seasons the same everywhere?

When you think of winter do you picture snow in your mind?
Or do you think of picnics at the beach?

Where you live determines what kind of spring, summer, autumn, and winter you have. If you live near the equator where the sun shines much of the time, winter and summer may not be very different. You would think of seasons as "rainy" and "dry" instead.

If you live farther north or south of the equator, the weather is very different during each of the four seasons.

10

Scientists study space in many ways.

How Do We Know About Objects in Space?

- Engage students in a discussion of how people learn about what is in space. Ask questions such as:

  "How do we know what is in space?" *(We look in the sky. We read books about space. We see videos.)*

  "Where do the books and videos come from?" *(Scientists and other people write about discoveries. Videos show pictures of the planets and moons.)*

  "It's a long way out to the planets and their moons. Who takes these pictures?" *(Space probes with cameras are sent out.)*

- Read sections about the tools astronomers use from books such as *Night Sky (Eyewitness Explorers)* by Carole Stott (Dorling Kindersley, 1993) and *Solar System (Interfact)* text by Jan Graham (World Book Inc., 1997).

Note: Many books on space have text that is too complex for primary students but have excellent pictures of the various space probes that can be shared.

Ask students to think of reasons why telescopes and space probes are important tools for astronomers. *(Telescopes make the planets seem closer. Space probes can go far out in space. Space probes can go places that are too far away for people to travel.)*

- Invite an astronomer to speak to your class about the tools he or she uses to study distant objects. Work with students to prepare a list of questions in advance. Follow up with thank-you letters.

- Make a page entitled "Astronomers Study Space" for the class logbook. Use copies of page 4 for students to write the information for individual logbooks.

Astronomers Study Space

Astronomers use big telescopes to study far off planets and stars.

Space probes fly by planets to study them.

The Russians put up a space station to study space.

A Space-Study Time Line

Work together to create an accordion-folded time line of space study. The time line will show stages of development rather than specific dates.

Materials

- reproduce page 79 for each student
- two 6" x 18" (15 x 45.5 cm) pieces of construction paper
- ruler and pencil
- scissors
- glue or tape

Steps to Follow

Prepare the accordion-folded paper.

1. Glue or tape the two sheets of construction paper together.
2. Follow these steps to fold the paper into sixths.
    a. Measure 6" (15 cm) from the left end. Draw a line. (You may need to do up through this step in advance for younger students.)
    b. Fold the paper along the line.
    c. Continue folding back and forth, using the first box as a guide.

3. Cut out and glue the pictures in chronological order on the inside sections of the time line. Discuss what each picture shows.
4. Write words or sentences on the chalkboard for students to copy.

sample words:	eyes
	telescope
	bigger telescopes
	astronauts on the moon
	space probes
	space vehicles on planets

sample sentences: Long, long ago people used just their eyes to study the sky.
Telescopes let people see some of the planets.
Bigger telescopes let astronomers study far-off planets.
Astronauts traveled to the moon. They brought back rocks and pictures.
Space probes have gone close to planets. They send back pictures.
A rover vehicle landed on Mars. It sent back pictures, too.

5. Students copy one phrase or sentence onto the correct sections of the time line.

Extension Activities

Family Night

Invite parents and their children to school one evening. Observe the stars, planets, and moons using eyes, binoculars, and telescopes. Have star charts available for identifying constellations. Invite an astronomer (professional or amateur) to answer questions and help identify objects in the sky.

Field Trip

• Take a field trip to an observatory or a planetarium. When you return to school, have students relate what they learned on the trip. Make a page for the class logbook entitled "A Trip to the Observatory."

• Reproduce page 80 for students to write about the trip for their individual logbooks.

A Trip to the Observatory

We went to the observatory.

An astronomer explained how a big telescope is used.

We went into a large room to see a show about planets and stars.

Note: Reproduce this page for each student to use with page 78.

Name ________________________________

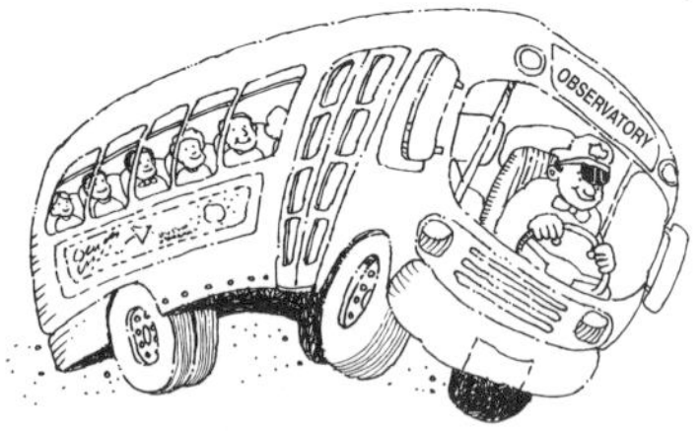

A Trip to the Observatory

What I saw:

What I learned: ________________________________